Getting Sara Married

A COMEDY

by

Sam Bobrick

SAMUEL FRENCH

FOUNDED 1830

NEW YORK HOLLYWOOD LONDON TORONTO

SAMUELFRENCH.COM

ISBN 978-0-573-66262-1   Printed in U.S.A.   #9217

IMPORTANT BILLING AND CREDIT
REQUIREMENTS

THE CAST

(In Order of Appearance)

SARA HASTINGS – An unmarried woman in her mid-thirties.

AUNT MARTHA – Sara's unpredictable aunt in her mid-sixties.

NOOGIE MALLOY – A very special delivery man in his late forties.

BRANDON CATES – A potential husband that Aunt Martha has picked out for Sara. In his mid-thirties.

HEATHER BOYD – Brandon's fiancée. In her mid-twenties.

THE CHIROPRACTOR – In his mid-thirties. A non-speaking part.

ACT I

Scene 1

TIME: *The present. A spring evening.*

PLACE: *The living room of Sara Hastings' one bedroom, east side luxury high rise apartment. The front door is at Stage Right. A door leading to the bedroom is at Upstage Left. A few feet down from there is a doorway leading to the kitchen. Along the Upstage Center wall is a large window flanked by two tall bookcases filled with legal books and several art pieces. The room is tastefully furnished. A sofa is at Stage Center flanked by two side chairs. A coffee table is in front of the sofa. Two end tables are at the sides of the sofa. On one of the side tables is a framed photo of Aunt Martha. An attractive desk and chair is at Stage Left just below the kitchen entrance. On the desk, among a pile of papers and books, there is a cordless phone and a laptop computer. At both downstage corners there is room for areas to be lit up as indicated in the play.*

AT RISE: **SARA HASTINGS,** *an attractive woman in her mid-thirties is busy at her desk working at her laptop computer. Her desk is cluttered. Near her is half a deli-delivered sandwich that she has been nibbling at since lunch. The PHONE RINGS. Without taking her eyes off of her work she picks it up and holds it by placing it between her ear and her shoulder.*

SARA. Yes?

(A corner area at Down Stage Right LIGHTS UP and we meet AUNT MARTHA, a woman in her mid-sixties. Dressed in a warm up suit, she speaks through a head set while lifting hand weights.)

AUNT MARTHA. Sara, it's Aunt Martha.

SARA. *(Not thrilled with the call)* Oh, hello, Aunt Martha. I was just going to call you.

AUNT MARTHA. No, you weren't.

SARA. Yes, I was.

AUNT MARTHA. No, you weren't.

SARA. Yes, I was.

AUNT MARTHA. No, you weren't.

SARA. Okay, I wasn't.

AUNT MARTHA. See! Do I know you or do I know you? Right now you're probably slaving away at your stupid computer with a half-eaten tuna salad sandwich that was supposed to be your lunch.

(Sara looks at her sandwich to make sure it's tuna salad)

SARA. Lucky guess.

AUNT MARTHA. Work, work, work. For what?

SARA. For food, for clothing, for shelter. For trying to live in New York a couple of steps above the poverty line.

AUNT MARTHA. And all the time letting life pass you by. What you should be doing with that dopey computer is checking all those internet dating services for a soul mate. Your cousin Jennifer found herself a husband that way and what a lovely man he is.

SARA. Yes. But before him she also found four serial killers. Please, Aunt Martha, I'd love to talk to you but I have three days to prepare for a trial and I don't want to go into court with a headache.

AUNT MARTHA. What about the Judge?

SARA. What Judge?

AUNT MARTHA. The one you're going to try your case in front of.

SARA. What about him?

AUNT MARTHA. Is he single?

SARA. I have no idea.

AUNT MARTHA. Is your client single?

SARA. My client is a lowlife, scumbag embezzler.

AUNT MARTHA. That's not what I asked you. Think about the future, Sara. You don't want to travel that long road of life alone. Everyone needs someone. And most of all…

SARA & AUNT MARTHA. Who's going to take care of you when you get sick?

AUNT MARTHA. Exactly. I worry about you, Sara. Left to your own devices, I fear you're going to end up an old maid. When I was your age I was already married twice.

SARA. I need to go, Aunt Martha. Unless there's something important…

AUNT MARTHA. Okay, I'll get right to the point. I'm determined that this year you're going to get married and so I've started the ball rolling on my own. Tonight there's going to be a fellow named Noogie stopping by.

SARA. Noogie? Aunt Martha there's never been a Noogie in my life and most likely it's because anyone with that name is in the penitentiary. Please tell me this Noogie is not someone you're trying to fix me up with.

AUNT MARTHA. No, no. Of course not. Noogie is…is well, Noogie is the delivery man.

SARA. The what?

(The DOORBELL rings)

Oh, God. There's someone at the door right now. Aunt Martha am I going to appreciate this?

AUNT MARTHA. Young people today appreciate very little. I'll hold on.

(The DOORBELL rings again)

SARA. I'm coming.

*(Sara puts the phone on the desk and goes to the door. Opens it a crack. **NOOGIE MALLOY**, a tough looking, but harmless man in his late 40's stands at the doorway.*

He is carrying a briefcase)

Yes?

NOOGIE. Sara Hastings?

SARA. It depends.

NOOGIE. I have something for you from your Aunt Martha.

(Hands her the brief case)

Can you hold this?

*(He then turns to the right side of the door and begins pulling in a large dolly. Strapped to it is **BRANDON CATES**, a nice looking, well dressed man in his mid-thirties and at this time, unconscious)*

Where do you want him?

SARA. Oh, my God!

NOOGIE. Please, there's nothing to worry about. He's going to be fine. He just got a slight bonk on the noggin. I'll just plop him down on the sofa.

SARA. I'm hallucinating. Please let me be hallucinating.

(During the following Noogie pushes the dolly to the sofa, unfastens his passenger and tilts the dolly so that Brandon falls to the sofa)

NOOGIE. Not to worry. I'm a total professional. The way I bonk 'em it hardly leaves a bruise. In fact it's almost beneficial. It actually clears the mind. Worries, anxieties, resentments, they all fly out the window. It sort of works like that meditation crap but I get you there a little faster.

(Noogie begins to prop Brandon up on the sofa)

Do you want him sitting up or lying down?

SARA. I want him in another apartment.

(Throws the briefcase on a chair and rushes to phone and picks it up)

Aunt Martha. Are you crazy?

AUNT MARTHA. Well, yes, a little bit. But aren't we all to some degree?

SARA. You sent me a...

AUNT MARTHA. Yes. Isn't he cute? His name is Brandon Cates and I've been trying to get you two together for months. But you resisted, he resisted. It was very frustrating so I was forced to take a different approach.

SARA. Aunt Martha, this time you have crossed over the line. Do you realize what you've done? You could go to prison for kidnapping.

AUNT MARTHA. No, not kidnapping. Matchmaking. Besides you're a lawyer. You'll see that I get a fair trial. People nowadays are very understanding when it comes to affairs of the heart.

SARA. This is insane.

AUNT MARTHA. No. It's innovative and I wouldn't be at all surprised if one day it ended up as a reality TV series.

NOOGIE. *(Putting a receipt in front of Sara and offering her a pen)* You want to sign this?

SARA. Absolutely not! I'm not signing anything.

(On phone)

Do you hear that, Aunt Martha? I'm not signing anything.

(Brandon begins moaning)

SARA *(CONTINUED)* He's moaning. He must be coming to. What do I do?

AUNT MARTHA. Well, I would start out with some small talk. You know, like what restaurants you like, what movies you've seen.

NOOGIE. I could put him under for a little longer if you need. Maybe you want to put on some make-up or something.

SARA. *(Annoyed at the suggestion)* You think I need make-up?

NOOGIE. Oh, no, no. Not at all, but you know you women. You like to have an edge.

(Brandon moans again)

SARA. *(Back on phone)* You know what's scary, Aunt Martha. I have your genes.

(Sara slams the phone down. LIGHTS OUT on Aunt Martha. Sara turns to Noogie)

I can't believe this. How did you get him here? There are people on the streets, there's a doorman downstairs.

NOOGIE. That's the beauty of New York. No one pays attention to anything. You really have your privacy. Now you want to sign this?

(Waves receipt in front of her again)

SARA. I said no!

NOOGIE. Your aunt said you're a difficult person.

SARA. My aunt was being kind.

NOOGIE. *(Hands her a business card)* Listen, if there's any further need for my services, here's my card. "Noogie Malloy Enterprises." I'm kind of a jack of all trades. If I can't do it, it can't be done.

SARA. Well, Noogie, you're going to be doing twenty years to life if you don't get out of here right now.

NOOGIE. Got'cha. Nice meeting you. I guess a tip is out of the question?

SARA. Out!

NOOGIE. Right.

(Passes Brandon)

He's a nice looking guy. Your aunt has very good taste.

(Noogie EXITS. Brandon moans again and begins to stir and sit up)

BRANDON. Oh, wow. What happened? Where am I?

SARA. You're fine. You're in my apartment. Stay right there. I'll get you some water.

(EXITS hurriedly to kitchen)

BRANDON. Yeah. Water. I'd like some. This is so weird. All I remember is leaving my office, getting on the elevator and then everything went black.

SARA. *(ENTERS quickly with a glass of water)* Really? Maybe it's that new flu that's going around. *nodding*

BRANDON. What new flu?

SARA. I don't know but there's always one going around.

(Hands him water)

Drink this.

BRANDON. You know what else is weird? Even though my mind feels extremely rested, much of my memory seems to have left me. I'm not sure I even know you.

SARA. No. No, you don't.

BRANDON. Then you don't know me?

SARA. No, not really. I mean, not at all.

BRANDON. And I'm in your apartment?

SARA. Yes.

BRANDON. And you just let me in without knowing who I am?

SARA. Basically, yes.

BRANDON. That wasn't very smart. I could be a maniac or something.

SARA. Obviously though, you're not.

BRANDON. Yes. Well, so far. Did I say anything at all when I came to your door?

SARA. Well, not really. You were actually quite out of it.

BRANDON. And you let me in?

SARA. Yes.

BRANDON. *You're* not a maniac by any chance?

SARA. No. Not yet.

BRANDON. Everything seems so vague. I can't seem to remember my name.

SARA. Well, I uh…I believe it's Brandon.

BRANDON. How do you know?

SARA. Well, I…I heard you moan something like that.

BRANDON. Really? Why would I moan my own name?

SARA. I asked the same question. But then we live in a very sexually progressive society and you can't be surprised by anything.

BRANDON. Brandon. That sounds...sort of right.

SARA. Why don't you look in your wallet. That might help bring things back.

BRANDON. Yes, my wallet. It's still here.

(Takes out wallet)

So obviously robbery wasn't the motive.

SARA. No, no, it wasn't.

BRANDON. How do you know?

SARA. Well, I uh, I don't. But you have your wallet. And your watch is still on your wrist. And uh, you have your shoes which is also a high risk item in this town. So obviously it wasn't robbery.

BRANDON. *(Looks in his wallet and ruffles through some bills)* You're right. Wow! There's four hundred dollars in here. I must be doing very well.

(Flips to wallet windows)

You're right again. My name is Brandon. Brandon Cates. I'm not too thrilled about the name Brandon but maybe I'll get to like it better as soon as things start coming back to me.

(Realizes something)

Oh, no.

SARA. What?

BRANDON. I think I'm a dentist.

SARA. Oh, a professional man. How nice.

BRANDON. No. Not at all. The thought of looking into mouths all day. What a turn off. And then when you lean your patient back you see so much nose hair and other stuff.

SARA. I guess it goes with the territory. Can I get you anything? Have you had dinner yet? I've got half a tuna salad sandwich. A bite's missing but it's okay. I had a check-up two weeks ago and I'm perfectly healthy.

BRANDON. Tuna? I'm not sure if I like tuna. Besides, I think we're having dinner.

SARA. We're?

BRANDON. Yes. I did say "we're" didn't I? Let me think. I believe I'm supposed to meet someone at the theatre tonight and then afterwards we were going out for… Oh-oh.

SARA. What?

BRANDON. Oh, my. Joan. I'm taking Joan to the theatre tonight.

SARA. Joan?

BRANDON. My fiancée?

SARA. *(Shocked)* You have a fiancée? *(Recovering)* I mean, you have a fiancée. How nice.

BRANDON. Yes. I believe I'm engaged. I think I'm actually getting married in a few months. I wonder what she looks like. What time is it?

SARA. It's a little after nine. You can probably still catch the second act, and if the first act isn't over, you could be the first one in the bathroom.

BRANDON. I have a feeling I'm always late for everything. That's the trouble with being a dentist. I'm constantly squeezing someone in with an emergency. It's either an impacted molar or a broken crown. I wonder if I do root canal. There's big money in that. You have very pretty teeth. You don't go to me, do you?

SARA. No. We don't know each other, remember?

BRANDON. That's right. Well, I'd better get down to the theater.

SARA. Yes, you'd better.

(Helping him to his feet)

BRANDON. But what theater? I haven't a clue what play we're seeing?

(Sticks his hands in his pocket and pulls out theatre ticket envelope)

Oh, no.

SARA. What?

BRANDON. I have the theatre tickets.

(Takes out tickets and looks at them)

"The Phantom of The Opera!" God, is that still running?

(Whistles)

Whoa! A hundred and twenty bucks a piece! I must really be in love. I need to call Joan. She probably went home.

(Sara picks up her phone)

SARA. I'll dial for you. What's her number?

BRANDON. I don't know. I can't remember that either.

SARA. I'll call information. What's her last name?

BRANDON. Yeah. Last name. Last name. Good question.

SARA. What about a cell phone? You have one?

BRANDON. I do.

SARA. I'm sure you must have her programmed in? Maybe scrolling through it might bring everything back.

BRANDON. Good idea.

(Spots briefcase)

My briefcase! My cell's in my briefcase.

(Picks up briefcase)

Oh, no. It's locked and I can't remember the combination.

SARA. No problem. I'll get a screwdriver and we'll pry it open.

BRANDON. No. I couldn't do that. It was a gift from Joan.

SARA. You remember that?

BRANDON. Not really, but it had to be. I'm a dentist. What do I need with a briefcase?

(Flustered)

Can I have some more water?

SARA. Oh, sure.

(Sara takes the glass and EXITS to the kitchen. Brandon puts the briefcase down and looks around)

BRANDON. Nice place.

SARA (O.S.) Thanks. I bought it two years ago.

BRANDON. I like it a lot. Very cozy, very practical. Just where is it located exactly?

SARA (O.S.) 78th and Madison.

BRANDON. The East side? How the heck did I get here? I believe my office is way downtown. *(Upset)* Oh. Oh, no.

SARA. *(ENTERS with glass of water)* What?

BRANDON. I'm not a dentist. I'm...I'm an insurance salesmen. I need to go to a dentist. I've been having trouble with a loose filling. An insurance salesman. That's even worse than a dentist isn't it?

SARA. Well, yes, as a rule.

(Hands Brandon water)

BRANDON. Hey, maybe that's why I'm up here, to sell you insurance. Were you interested in term or full life with a big cash payment when you check out?

SARA. Actually, I'm fine with my insurance plan. Maybe you'd like some aspirin with the water?

BRANDON. No. I'd better not. It's possible I could be allergic to it. On all the insurance forms they ask what medicines you're allergic to. It helps the company know what the chances of your being saved are in case you come down with something potentially fatal.

(Drinks water)

Hey, maybe you need a good hospitalization plan? I think I might have something with a low deductible and a high coverage.

SARA. Thanks, but I'm perfectly fine with what I have. Besides, the premiums have skyrocketed so much it's actually starting to make sense to just die.

BRANDON. Doesn't it. Okay, let's try to back track again. I'm an insurance salesman. I work downtown. I'm going to the theater on the West side. I end up on the East side. In what seems to be a very nice building, in a very desirable neighborhood, obviously close to transportation and...Oh-oh.

SARA. Now what?

BRANDON. What a relief. I'm not an insurance salesman after all.

SARA. Job stability doesn't seem to be your strong point. So what do you do now?

BRANDON. I'm in real estate. Because of my bad crown I was going to check into my dental insurance plan so that's why insurance was on my mind. I'm so glad not to be in that business. You can't believe the phony claims people make.

SARA. I know. Whiplash has paid for more Hawaiian vacations than anyone cares to admit.

BRANDON. Yes, yes, I'm a real estate salesman. That's why I was so impressed with this apartment. There's so much crap on the market that when you finally discover something nice you're very excited.

SARA. Well, I hope you enjoy that line of work more than you did dentistry and insurance.

BRANDON. Well, no, I really don't. You can't imagine the difficult people I have to deal with. Especially couples getting married. One wants a fireplace, one wants a skylight. They agree on nothing. It's kind of sad to see some of these relationships in action and know that they're absolutely doomed. You're not married, right?

SARA. How can you tell?

BRANDON. The way your place is decorated. Nothing clashes. No compromises had to be made. No Lazy-Boy lounge chair, no 52 inch TV screen with Dolby Surround Sound. All this space is yours. I think the hardest thing about getting married is resigning yourself to the fact that you're actually letting an intruder into your life.

SARA. Hopefully you and Joan worked out that problem?

BRANDON. I hope so. Anyway, I really like this place and just in case you decide to sell, keep me in mind. I'll even lower my commission. I wonder if I have a card.

(Searches pocket)

No, no I don't. I'll send you one. Oh, gee. Forgive me. All the time I've been here, I never asked you your name.

SARA. It's Sara. Sara Hastings.

BRANDON. That's a very pretty name, Sara. Well Sara Hastings, thanks for...wait a minute. Hastings, Hastings. I think I know someone with that last name. I'm almost sure I do. Let me think.

SARA. *(Attempting to change the subject)* So, you're getting married. You must be very excited.

BRANDON. Yes. I'll bet I am.

(Spots a picture of Aunt Martha on an end table)

Hey. Who's this? I think I know her.

SARA. Oh, uh, her. Uh that's uh...

BRANDON. Wait, wait. I've got it. Martha. Martha Hastings. Yes. Of course I know her. That's where I know the name Hastings from. She's one of my clients. Oh... Oh, gosh. What a relief. I'm not in real estate either.

SARA. No?

BRANDON. I'm a financial advisor. Wonderful occupation. Very high powered. I deal in stocks, bonds, mutual funds...By any chance do you know how the market did today?

SARA. I really don't.

BRANDON. Just as well. You'll live longer. Yes, I'm a financial advisor. Martha is one of my clients. Oh, gosh. That picture brought it all back. I'm with Gurney and Gurney. Wonderful company. The second Gurney is dead. I'm being groomed to replace him. Oh, wow. I have a great future and I think I take two hours for lunch.

(Looks at Aunt Martha's picture again)

Yeah. Martha Hastings. It's starting to come back.

SARA. *(Pulls the picture away from Brandon)*

Well, Brandon, you probably need to be on your way.

BRANDON. I know. I'd just like to see that picture again if I may.

(Pulls the picture back from Sara)

SARA. Well, I uh, it's not a very good picture of her. She's actually much taller.

BRANDON. *(Studying the picture)* Yes. Martha Hastings. Persistent little lady. She always keeps telling me about this niece of hers she wants me to…Wait a minute. You…you're not…you're not…

SARA. I'm afraid I am.

BRANDON. So that's why I'm here. To see you. But why? I'm engaged. How do you like that? I'm not even married and I'm already cheating. What a rat I turned out to be. Why would your aunt want to fix you up with a lowlife like me?

SARA. You're not a lowlife. You're not cheating. We never met before. You had no intention of coming here and I never heard your name mentioned until…until…

BRANDON. Yes, I know. Until I moaned it myself. I don't know. Something just doesn't add up. Actually you're quite attractive. Your Aunt Martha was working so hard to get us together that I was sure you weren't. Maybe I shouldn't have brushed her off.

SARA. But you're engaged, remember?

BRANDON. Well, I am now, but I wasn't when your aunt started in on me. Actually, until she started in on me, I was a confirmed bachelor. But she kept on and on about…

SARA. How important it was not to travel that long road of life alone.

BRANDON. Yes.

SARA. And how everybody needs somebody.

BRANDON. That too.

SARA. And worst of all, who's going to take care of you when you're sick.

BRANDON. That was the killer. She wore me down so much that when Joan came into my life, well, I was practically a sitting duck.

SARA. So actually, my aunt is responsible for your being engaged. She'll be so thrilled to hear this.

BRANDON. Trust me, I had to overcome some major issues. But like the Chinese say, the journey of a thousand miles begins with a single step.

SARA. I know. You just have to be sure you're not on the edge of the Grand Canyon when you take it.

BRANDON. I'm pretty sure I'll be okay with Joan. She's a terrific girl, not at all demanding, extremely understanding. I think things are going quite nicely with us except Joan is...is...is...

SARA. Is what?

BRANDON. Is really Heather.

SARA. There is no Joan?

BRANDON. Well, yes, there is except she's our real estate agent. That's probably why I thought I was in real estate. Wow, so many things are popping back in my head. It's like discovering the world all over again. Anyway, my fiancée's name is Heather. Heather Bangor.

SARA. I'll bet she'll be happy to change her last name.

BRANDON. You'd think. No, wait. That's where she's from. Bangor, Maine. It's Boyd. Heather Boyd. We met...I can't quite remember. Oh, yes. My dentist fixed me up. She's one of his patients. She works for an insurance company. Look how everything ties up so nicely.

SARA. And Joan, the real estate agent is helping you two look for an apartment.

BRANDON. Uh huh. I have to admit she has the patience of a saint because what I like...

SARA. Heather doesn't like.

BRANDON. Yes. And what Heather likes…

SARA. You're not that crazy about.

BRANDON. Yes, but Joan assures us it's not that uncommon. Gosh, I've been talking so much, I think I worked up a bit of an appetite. Maybe I will have that half of a sandwich you offered me.

SARA. Oh, sure.

BRANDON. You're definitely not going to eat it?

SARA. Positive.

(Hands him the sandwich)

BRANDON. Thanks.

(Bites into it)

I wonder if Heather would like a place like this? It's hard to tell. I should call her. If only I could remember her number. Gosh, maybe I had a stroke.

SARA. You're a bit young for that.

BRANDON. Really. How old do you think I am?

SARA. I'd say mid-thirties.

BRANDON. Oh, that's nice. Mid-thirties. Then it's time I did get married. I'm probably a lot more settled down now than I was in my twenties. Any guy in your life?

SARA. No.

BRANDON. That's too bad.

SARA. It's my choice.

BRANDON. Oh, I'm sure it is. A pretty girl like you. But I should warn you. Marriage is one of those things that the longer you run away from it, the more fearful it becomes.

SARA. You're obviously speaking about yourself.

BRANDON. I'm not sure. It's just something that just popped into my head. I'm starting to get a better fix on Heather. She's a bit younger than me. Almost seven years. But she's very mature for her age. Loves foreign movies and wears a lot of brown.

(Recalling more)

330-720-7341. Yes, that's it. 330-720-7341. That's Heather's number.

SARA. I'll dial it for you.

BRANDON. No. Don't. I'm wrong. That's my social security number. Wait, there's something else I'm starting to remember.

(Takes a bit out of the sandwich)

This sandwich...What kind did you say it was?

SARA. Tuna salad.

BRANDON. Tuna salad. Oh-oh.

SARA. Now what.

BRANDON. I'm deadly allergic to tuna.

(Puts down sandwich, grasps his throat and sits back on a chair)

Quick. Dial 9-1-1...Hurry! Hurry! My throat is closing. I can't breathe. Hurry!

SARA. *(She frantically grabs the phone and begins dialing)* Right.

BRANDON. Hurry!

SARA. I am! I am!

BRANDON. I also think...

SARA. Yes?

BRANDON. The sandwich...

SARA. Yes?

BRANDON. Not enough mayo.

(Gasping, Brandon topples over on the sofa as Sara looks on in horror)

BLACKOUT

End of Act I, Scene 1

Scene 2

TIME: The next morning. Brandon is asleep on the sofa with a blanket over him. Sara is at her desk on the phone to Aunt Martha, who is in her Down Stage Right corner wearing her head set and peddling a stationary bike.

AUNT MARTHA. Tuna Fish? Poor guy. He doesn't know what he's missing. There's nothing better than tuna salad on rye with a slice of tomato. Some people have no luck.

SARA. Aunt Martha, not that it matters, but why in the world would you want to fix me up with someone who's already engaged?

AUNT MARTHA. Because I liked him and I thought he would like you and as a wedding gift I'd be willing to buy out the other woman. Besides, he's not getting married for several months so we have a nice window of opportunity.

SARA. Obviously you still don't realize the seriousness of this situation. Listen to me, Aunt Martha. You can go to jail. We can both go to jail. We are involved in a crime.

AUNT MARTHA. Oh, grow up. We are involved in the pursuit of love. If the police start locking up well meaning people like us, where will they find room for all the real criminals, the robbers, the killers and almost every politician.

SARA. Aunt Martha, are you on drugs? Get this through that warped mind of yours. Knocking guys over the head and dragging them off is not an acceptable legal mating process.

AUNT MARTHA. Well, it worked with the cavemen and I guarantee you they had a much lower divorce rate than what we've got now.

SARA. Do me a favor, Aunt Martha, and stop thinking because the noise in your head is starting to get to me. A man almost died in my apartment last night. The paramedics said if I didn't give him mouth to mouth resuscitation they weren't sure if he would have lived.

AUNT MARTHA. You mean your lips have already met? How encouraging and it's only the first date. Anyway, even though I know it's going to work out with you and Brandon, if for some reason it doesn't, I've got my eye on this new chiropractor that I'm going to. He does wonders with his hands. In some areas you might like him better than Brandon.

(Brandon begins to moan and stir)

SARA. Aunt Martha, do you have the yellow pages handy?

AUNT MARTHA. They're not too far away.

SARA. Good. Look up the word "psychiatrist" and the first name you come to, go see him.

(Sara hangs up. LIGHTS OUT on Aunt Martha. Sara goes to Brandon)

BRANDON. *(Sitting up)* Where am I?

SARA. You're still here.

BRANDON. Right. Which is where?

SARA. My apartment. I'm Sara Hastings. We met last night, sort of.

BRANDON. Last night. Yes. I'm starting to remember. I walked out of my office, into the elevator and then I woke up here.

SARA. So far so good.

BRANDON. Then we talked a little bit. It seemed like pleasant conversation and then I had a tuna fish sandwich.

SARA. Yes.

BRANDON. This may sound crazy, but did someone pump something into my body last night?

SARA. The paramedics. They pumped air into your lungs. Part of the procedure.

BRANDON. And I faintly remember getting mouth to mouth.

SARA. *(Reluctantly)* Yes, you got that too.

BRANDON. From one of the paramedics?

SARA. Uh, probably one of them.

BRANDON. Male or female?

SARA. They were both males.

BRANDON. Why, am I thinking he was a good kisser? That's sick, isn't it? I really need to go. By any chance you wouldn't happen to have a cup of coffee around, would you?

SARA. The paramedics said your first meal should be something very easy. Like oatmeal and herbal tea.

BRANDON. Oh, well, I can probably pick that up on my way...

SARA. No. No I have it for you. I had it sent up from the deli around the corner. I just need to warm the oatmeal in the microwave and the tea is a matter of boiling water which I think I've almost mastered.

BRANDON. You can't cook?

SARA. I probably can. I just chose not to. It never really interested me and frankly with all the terrific restaurants in the city it's slowly becoming a lost art anyway.

BRANDON. Well, since our engagement, Heather made up her mind to conquer the kitchen. In fact, tonight she's preparing dinner for her parents and myself. She's actually making something from a cookbook. That kind of effort tells you a lot about a woman.

SARA. Yes. She can read. By the way, your briefcase rang twice during the night. I think you'd better call her. I'll go warm up your oatmeal.

(Sara EXITS to kitchen.)

BRANDON. Right.

(Takes the briefcase and begins fidgeting with the combination. Aloud to Sara)

Heather is quite committed to marriage. I guess I am too. It's really the normal progression of the human experience...

(Low and somewhat to himself)

…as my therapist explained to me.

(Aloud to Sara)

It's a definite sign of maturing. I remember the day I asked her to marry me…

(Low and to himself again)

…I felt so old.

SARA (O.S.) I'm sorry. I can't hear you.

BRANDON. Just as well.

(The briefcase snaps open)

SARA. *(ENTERS with a glass of water)* The tea and oatmeal are on their way. Maybe you should have some water first so you don't get dehydrated.

(Hands Brandon the water)

BRANDON. Thanks. I got my briefcase open. Easy combination. 1-2-3-4. I guess I'm not a very complicated person.

(Takes the water from Sara, drinks and hands her back the glass)

Delicious water. I'd better give Heather a call.

SARA. That might be wise.

BRANDON. *(Takes out his cell phone and speed dials)* Your aunt said you're a lawyer.

SARA. I am.

BRANDON. What kind of law?

SARA. Oh, a little of this, a little of that. Some litigation, some family law, some criminal law. Maybe soon, a kidnapping case.

BRANDON. *(Indicating phone)* It's ringing. She's most likely at home. She was planning to take the day off because of the dinner tonight. In a way I dread the evening. Her parents are very difficult to make conversation with. They mostly just stare at me.

SARA. Well, you said they're from Maine. They probably don't get to see very many people.

(The MICROWAVE BEEPS)

That's your oatmeal. Be right back.

(She EXITS to kitchen)

BRANDON. Thanks.

(We hear Heather's PHONE RING. The Down Stage Left corner LIGHTS UP and **HEATHER BOYD** *answers the phone. Heather is a very attractive looking woman in her mid-twenties. She is wearing an apron. She is always dressed in various shades of brown)*

HEATHER. Yes?

BRANDON. Heather. It's me Brandon.

HEATHER. Oh, Brandon, sweetheart. Thank goodness. Are you all right?

BRANDON. Yes, yes, I'm fine.

HEATHER. I called your cell, I called the police, I checked with the hospitals. I even called the morgue. What happened to you?

BRANDON. Well, it's so bizarre, I'm not sure you're going to believe it.

HEATHER. Of course I will, sweetheart.

BRANDON. Good. Well, last night when I left my office, I got on the elevator and the next thing I remember is waking up several hours later in some strange woman's apartment. I mean, the woman wasn't strange, she was actually quite friendly, uh...nurturing...uh caring...

(With silence from Heather he realizes he must come up with less threatening language)

How about concerned? Yes, that's the word. She was very concerned.

HEATHER. Was she? And where are you now?

BRANDON. Well, uh, I'm still in her apartment. I would have called you last night but, see I ate part of her tuna fish sandwich and passed out and didn't get up until this morning. She's making oatmeal for me now. What a terrific apartment she has. I think you should see it. It might give you a few ideas.

HEATHER. Really. Well, I think I already have them, Brandon.

(Heather slams the phone down. LIGHTS OUT on Heather)

BRANDON. Heather? Heather.

(He dials again. LIGHTS UP on Heather as she answers the phone.)

HEATHER. How old is she?

BRANDON. Who?

HEATHER. This *friendly, nurturing, caring, concerned* woman whose terrific apartment you woke up in?

BRANDON. Wait a minute, when I said it, it didn't come out that suggestive. Oh, come on. You don't think for one minute that I'd…

HEATHER. Just answer the question.

BRANDON. Well, she's…She's probably in her…her seventies, maybe eighties.

HEATHER. Really?

(Sara ENTERS with a tray carrying the oatmeal and tea)

SARA. *(Softly but loud enough for Heather to hear)* I hope the oatmeal tastes okay. I was only able to nuke it for a couple of minutes because the plastic container it came in started to melt.

HEATHER. Was that her?

BRANDON. Yes.

HEATHER. You say she's eighty?

BRANDON. Every day of it.

HEATHER. I don't think so.

(She slams the phone down again. LIGHTS OUT on Heather)

BRANDON. Heather! Heather! Heather!

(Brandon is embarrassed that it's so obvious Heather has hung up on him. He quickly puts the phone away)

These damn cell phones. It's so hard to pick up a signal, sometimes.

SARA. She hung up.

BRANDON. No, we were cut off.

SARA. She hung up. What did you tell her that she didn't believe?

BRANDON. That you were seventy.

SARA. Big mistake. A woman knows when a man's lying. That's why I try to get more men on a jury when I have a client with an improbable story. We women have certain intuitive gifts that a man doesn't possess. It must have been given to us to level the playing field.

BRANDON. I didn't want to give her any irrational thoughts about my staying here overnight.

SARA. Well, she certainly has a few now. Would you like me to call her? As I mentioned, I also do a little family law and I have to mediate sticky situations all the time.

BRANDON. No. I'm afraid your getting involved might make matters worse.

SARA. Why would you say that?

BRANDON. Well, you know how women are. You'll talk, she'll talk, you'll both get friendly, you'll make a lunch date, she'll see how pretty you are and boom, I'll be in the dog house again. Anyway, a dozen long stemmed roses and it will all smooth itself out.

SARA. That's the formula?

BRANDON. *(Begins eating the oatmeal)* No, that's the antidote. I hope I haven't made her sound difficult. She's really not. Sometimes I think guys have a way of getting into hot water even when there's no reason for it. Very good oatmeal. You can hardly taste the plastic.

SARA. Thank you.

BRANDON. I'm still very curious why I ended up here. Your aunt never told me where you live.

SARA. She didn't? Well, maybe she did and you just can't remember yet. Anyway in your weakened condition you should give your brain a rest. A good bonk on the head can sometimes take months before everything starts to clear up.

BRANDON. What makes you think I was bonked on the head?

SARA. Oh, well, I...I...I'm still only guessing. It's most likely you may have just walked into something or maybe something fell on you. These old buildings have air conditioners that tumble out of the windows all the time.

BRANDON. *(Rubbing his head)* You could be right about my being bonked. I can feel a slight bump. Do you think I ought to report this incident to the police?

SARA. *(Quickly)* No.

BRANDON. No?

SARA. I mean...Well, let's face it. What could you tell them?

BRANDON. Actually, not much.

SARA. And what do you expect them to do with that information?

BRANDON. Yeah, you're right. It would just be a lot of red tape for nothing. I guess I'll just forget it.

SARA. I hope so. I mean, I hope so...you never have this trouble again. I don't see why you should.

BRANDON. Well, I'd better get going home. I need to wash up and get down to my office. I can't thank you enough for what you've done for me. Taking me in, calling the paramedics...

SARA. You didn't finish your oatmeal. I didn't warm it up properly?

BRANDON. No, no, you did. It was the best warmed up anything I ever had. I wouldn't lose that formula. It works. I just need to get going.

(Starts to gathers his things)

Anyway, your aunt was right about you. You are a very special girl.

SARA. That's how she described me? Special? What a lame word.

BRANDON. It is, isn't it. Maybe that's why I wasn't interested. You'd be smart to give her some photos to show around. That would make a big difference.

(He opens the front door, then turns and extends his hand to her)

Goodbye.

SARA. *(Shaking his hand)* Goodbye.

(He starts to close the door then turns to Sarah again)

BRANDON. Listen, are you sure it was a male paramedic that gave me the mouth to mouth?

SARA. Positive.

BRANDON. Hmmm. Strange.

(He EXITS closing the door behind him. Sara stands there for a beat looking at the closed door then turns to the audience in thought)

SARA. Yes. Isn't it?

LIGHTS SLOWLY FADE

End of Act I, Scene 2

Scene 3

TIME: That evening. Sara is on the phone and looking over several papers. A peanut butter and jelly sandwich is on a plate on her desk.

SARA. Listen, Lou, I'm not halfway through our client's records and it looks like he's an even bigger liar and thief than we thought. You need to talk to him about changing his plea. No, guilty isn't enough. *Real* guilty is more like it.

(SOUND: DOORBELL)

There's someone at the door. I'll talk to you later. Anyway, it's going to be a tougher case than we thought.

(Hangs up. Without taking her eyes off the papers, she walks to the door and opens it. It's Noogie. He's holding Brandon's briefcase and hands it to Sara)

NOOGIE. Hi.

SARA. Oh, no.

(Noogie ENTERS the apartment, once again pulling in a somewhat unconscious Brandon strapped to the dolly)

NOOGIE. You want him in the same place?

SARA. Tell me, I'm hallucinating.

(She puts the briefcase on a chair)

NOOGIE. I would have been here sooner but there were no cabs around. I had to take the subway.

SARA. With him? You took the subway with him?

NOOGIE. Yeah. That's why I was so late. It was murder getting him through the turnstile.

(The PHONE RINGS. Sara answers it as Noogie unties Brandon and tips him to the sofa)

SARA. *(On phone. Sharply)* What?

(Down Stage Right corner LIGHTS UP on Aunt Martha. She is on her head set, seated on a stool and holding a guitar)

AUNT MARTHA. How did you know it was me?

SARA. By the phone ring. It's very troubled. Anyway, yes, he's here and Noggie's here and you're just very lucky you're not here. You don't listen to me, do you Aunt Martha?

AUNT MARTHA. Well, truthfully, I try not to.

SARA. I can't talk to you. I need to go.

AUNT MARTHA. When should I call back?

SARA. How about after your third year in Sing-Sing.

(She slams her phone down)

AUNT MARTHA. I think she's softening.

(LIGHTS OUT on Aunt Martha)

NOOGIE. *(Approaches Sara with a receipt)* You want to sign this?

SARA. *(Point to door)* I'm counting to ten, Noggie.

NOOGIE. I did give you my card, didn't I?

SARA. One!

NOOGIE. Let me leave you a few more of them.

(He lays some cards on her desk)

I've been passing them out everywhere. I expect to get very busy once word gets around about the quality of my work.

SARA. Two!

NOOGIE. Jeez. You're very unreasonable. No wonder you're not married.

SARA. Seven!

NOOGIE. I'm going, I'm going.

(Indicates Brandon)

Look he's smiling. I think he's happy to be back.

(He EXITS. Brandon begins moaning)

BRANDON. Oh, man. Where am I?

SARA. I wish I wasn't the one to have to tell you.

BRANDON. Sara? I'm back at your place again?

SARA. I'm afraid so. I'll get you some water?

(Sara EXITS to kitchen)

BRANDON. It happened exactly the same way. I left my office, stepped into the elevator and then...and then here I am. I think this is more than just a coincidence, Sara. We need to figure this out.

(Rubbing head)

And this little lump on my head seems bigger than it was yesterday.

SARA. *(Returning with water)* Drink this.

(She hands it to Brandon who drinks)

BRANDON. The good news is I don't feel as disoriented as I did before. What time is it?

SARA. About nine thirty.

BRANDON. Oh, no. I was suppose to have dinner with Joan and her parents at eight.

SARA. That's Heather and her parents. Joan is your real estate agent.

BRANDON. You're right. So maybe my clarity isn't that good. But you know when I went into work today I never felt so serene. My mind didn't seem as cluttered and I didn't feel as anxious about things.

SARA. So you're saying that all-in-all this hasn't been a bad experience? Good. That'll be part of our defense.

BRANDON. Huh?

SARA. I'm sorry. I was just thinking aloud about a more than likely upcoming case.

(She hands him his briefcase)

You'd better call Heather.

BRANDON. Right.

(Enters combination)

1-2-3-4.

(The briefcase snaps open. During the following he takes out his cell phone and speed dials)

Her parents must be steamed. They're not too happy with me to begin with. For some reason every time I'm with them I fall asleep.

(We hear the PHONE DIAL. Down Stage Left LIGHTS UP on Heather. She is wearing an appropriate brown dress)

HEATHER. Hello?

BRANDON. *(On phone)* Heather? Listen, I'm so sorry about dinner.

HEATHER. *(Annoyed)* Where are you? I've called and called. We've been waiting for you for an hour and a half.

BRANDON. You'll never believe it. I'm back at Sara's.

HEATHER. Who?

BRANDON. That...uh seventy year old woman who's place I was at last night. By the way, did you get my flowers? I was also planning to pick up a little gold bracelet for you.

(Heather hangs up. Her area goes DARK)

BRANDON *(CONTINUED)* I'm doing something wrong.

(Puts his cell phone in his jacket pocket)

SARA. The gold bracelet. It had guilt written all over it.

BRANDON. I guess I'd better get over there and straighten things out.

(Drinks water)

These blackouts are really starting to concern me. I wonder if it's psychological? I hope subconsciously I'm not trying to avoid anything.

SARA. You mean like your upcoming marriage?

BRANDON. I don't know. I absolutely want to marry Heather because she's a terrific girl and I doubt I could ever do better than her. Of course I have to admit the decision took a lot more than just having your aunt hammer on me. But I thought I licked that.

SARA. With therapy?

BRANDON. No. Visualization. I would lie awake at night and visualize what married life would really be like.

SARA. How sweet.

BRANDON. Not really. You see I visualized it at it's very worst.

SARA. Why?

BRANDON. Because it would be a total fairy tale if I visualized it at it's very best. I thought if I could deal with it at it's very worst, then I'd have nothing to fear.

SARA. Interesting concept.

BRANDON. I thought so. Anyway, I start the process by first visualizing myself in the stronghold of a man's privacy.

SARA. The bathroom.

BRANDON. Exactly. I've just awakened and as I walk in, I come face to face with strange undergarments hanging all around. Bras, panties, nylons. Get the picture?

SARA. Every morning.

BRANDON. Next, I go to the shower and turn it on.

SARA. And?

BRANDON. It's cold. Ice cold. She got their first and used all the hot water.

SARA. Well, be fair. By the time she shampoos her hair and shaves her legs...

BRANDON. I got the picture. From the bathroom I go to the kitchen. The walk is not pleasant.

SARA. The reason being?

BRANDON. I have to pass through the living room which is now filled with pictures of all her relatives. Her mother, her father, her aunts, her uncles, her brother, her nephews, friends of her nephews, most of them, since the wedding, I've grown to hate. Next, breakfast. I go to the refrigerator and open it. Half of it is filled with lime Jell-O.

SARA. Obviously there's a weight problem.

BRANDON. Obviously. The reason being what's in the other half of the refrigerator. Baby formula.

SARA. You had a baby?

BRANDON. Seems that way. I start back towards my bedroom now noticing that this nice, wonderful, hip New York apartment that I once inhabited by myself and loved with all my heart is now crammed with a high chair, a crib, a bouncy chair, a baby swing, a baby buggy, a play pen, a humidifier and several hundred Beanie babies that are now covered from head to toe with everything a baby can spit up.

SARA. Moving on.

BRANDON. Right. I get out of there as fast as I can and go off to work, my jacket smelling from vomit because unbeknownst to me, Brandon junior threw up on it when I picked him up to kiss him goodbye. The smell stays in the jacket forever.

SARA. I think I once sat next to you on the subway.

BRANDON. One day I come home from work and in the middle of the bedroom is a pile of my favorite old clothes that my wife has decided to throw out because I haven't worn them in weeks and she needs the closet space.

SARA. The reason being?

BRANDON. The new baby. It seems if you can make one, you can make two which mean we now need...

SARA. A bigger place?

BRANDON. Exactly. So now I have to give up my nice, wonderful, hip New York apartment and move out to the suburbs, a million miles away, from my favorite restaurants, my terrific gym, the young girl at Starbucks who pours my coffee every morning, the excitement, the pace, the energy of the city I truly love.

SARA. Be reasonable. Changes had to be made.

BRANDON. Along the way she makes me get rid of my great little sports car that I used to drive up to the Hamptons on summer weekends before I was married. I am now forced to own one of those stupid clunky SUV's which soon fills up with the same baby crap my wonderful little New York apartment was filled with. In no time at all, every inch of upholstery is covered with crusted slobber and sticky kiddy goo. In fact, from now on, everything I touch seems covered with crusted slobber and sticky kiddy goo.

SARA. Brandon, you are now beginning to get a little too grim.

BRANDON. As the kids get bigger my space grows smaller. Now there are bicycles and wagons and scooters and skate boards and bunk beds and drum sets and car pools and Little League and soccer practice, and every day it takes a little bit longer to drive up and back to work because every day there's more cars on the highway because every day there's more guys like me getting married and I'm always rushing and always late and now we have six kids and life becomes more hectic and jammed and cramped and I suddenly realize I haven't seen my wife naked in fifteen years because three of our six kids are still sleeping in our bedroom. Besides, my wife has no time for sex because she's busy twenty four hours a day figuring out how to put more of her stuff in my closet space.

SARA. That's it! Stop! Quit! No more! I have never, never, ever heard anything more disparaging in my life. After that narrative even a polygamist wouldn't want to get married.

BRANDON. I know. But you see this was a worst case scenario. Odds are in my favor it could never be this dreadful. Once I realized that, it helped me get over the hump.

SARA. I can see why my aunt likes you. You make less sense than she does. By any chance you didn't let Heather in on this, did you?

BRANDON. No. Should I?

SARA. Only if you want to scare the hell out of her forever. Trust me, Brandon, you lay this visualization babble on her and she'll be out of your life in two seconds flat. For god's sake, you're trying to talk yourself into marriage not the death penalty. Think happiness, joy, romance, love.

BRANDON. Is that what you would think?

SARA. No. I would not think anything. I'm not in the marriage market.

BRANDON. Because?

SARA. Because at this point in my life I don't want a man in my life.

BRANDON. Because?

SARA. Because at this point in my life I don't need a man in my life.

BRANDON. Because?

SARA. Say, "because" one more time, Brandon and I'm going to punch your lights out.

BRANDON. I'm sorry. I didn't mean to upset you. I'm just curious to see what you're running away from to make sure I've covered that base.

SARA. Running away? One thing you'd better know about me. I'm not the kind to run away from anything. Let me tell you one thing I've learned from practicing law. Marriage is not the answer to happiness. In fact, most of the time divorce does the job a lot better.

(She picks up her sandwich and takes a bite)

BRANDON. I've upset you, haven't I? I'm sorry.

SARA. Good.

BRANDON. I honestly didn't mean to.

SARA. Well you did.

BRANDON. I guess I should go.

SARA. *(Coldly)* Take care.

(She returns to her work)

BRANDON. I feel bad leaving you on such a sour note.

SARA. I'll get over it.

BRANDON. *(Uneasy. Indicates Sara's sandwich)* That isn't another tuna fish sandwich is it?

SARA. No. It's peanut butter and jelly. I made it myself. For some stupid reason I've decided to expand my cooking horizons.

BRANDON. Peanut butter and jelly. I haven't had one of those since I was a kid. Do you think maybe I could have…

SARA. Brandon, Heather has a big meal waiting for you.

BRANDON. I know. But I am kind of hungry now. Maybe to hold me over I could have that other half of yours if you don't mind.

SARA. *(Hands him half of her sandwich)* Okay, here. Chew fast and leave.

BRANDON. Thanks. I'm really sorry I got you so upset.

SARA. Okay. You already said that.

BRANDON. Well, I'm not going to bother you anymore. At least I'm going to try not to bother you, which is another thing that bothers me, why I keep bothering you. I mean showing up here like I do, it doesn't make any sense.

SARA. *(Picks up some papers)* Brandon, I need to get back to a case I'm working on.

BRANDON. I'm sorry. I'll just finish this and go.

SARA. Good.

BRANDON. *(Biting into the sandwich)* This sandwich is delicious.

SARA. Thank you. Making it was a major achievement in my life.

BRANDON. You wouldn't happen to have some milk would you? I remembered how wonderful peanut butter and jelly tastes with milk.

SARA. I don't have any milk.

BRANDON. Too bad. You should drink milk. Calcium. Very good for your bones. Especially as a person ages… Gets older.

SARA. You know, Brandon, you are really turning this day into a piece of crap for me.

BRANDON. I'm sorry. I didn't mean older, older. I meant older as...in...I've upset you even more. Well, I'll just finish this sandwich and I'll go.

SARA. You keep saying that.

BRANDON. *(A beat)* Maybe you'd like to come to the wedding?

SARA. Whose?

BRANDON. Mine and Heather's.

SARA. No thanks.

BRANDON. Why not?

SARA. Because at this particular time I don't want to buy you a gift.

BRANDON. That's what I like about you. You're totally up front. You hide nothing. You should have been a guy. I wouldn't be surprised if you'd be my best friend.

SARA. I refuse to talk to you anymore.

BRANDON. I understand.

(Takes another bite of his sandwich)

Well, I guess I'll be going.

SARA. Ta ta.

BRANDON. I really upset you. Frankly, it's because I think I got you thinking about things. You're apparently just as frightened about marriage as I was.

SARA. Listen, if anyone has a hang-up about marriage, it's obviously still you. You're supposed to be at your fiancée's and look at the way you're stalling here. It's pretty damn clear to me that even though you think you've come to terms with the concept of matrimony you are still scared shitless.

BRANDON. I've upset you, haven't I?

SARA. Brandon, the next time you say that you're going to leave here with a shoe implant that's going to make sitting very uncomfortable. You want to know why *I'm* not into marriage? Because I find most men to be a giant pain in the ass. From the time I can remember,

I've had to fight with them over something. As a kid it was over teasing. In high school it was over my virginity. In Law school it was over grades. In court it's over cases and clients and settlements and at the end of the day, I'm so happy to be away from them, trust me, marriage, relationships, even dinners with them are the farthest thing from my mind.

(Bites into her sandwich)

BRANDON. What about sex?

SARA. Not while I'm eating. Goodnight, Brandon.

BRANDON. *(Stuffs the rest of the sandwich in his mouth)* You're right. I need to go. Well, thanks again for everything and… *(Starts gasping)* Oh, oh.

SARA. What? What?

BRANDON. *(Pointing to his throat)* It's closing up…My… throat's…closing up again.

SARA. No. Please, God, no.

BRANDON. I…I can't…I can't…I think it's the…the peanut butter. You'd better dial 9-1-1. Hurry! Hurry!

(He then collapses on sofa)

SARA. Goddamn it, Brandon! Can't you eat anything?

BLACK OUT

End of Act I

ACT II

Scene 1

TIME: The next morning. Brandon is once again asleep on the sofa with a blanket over him. His jacket is hung over the back of a chair. Sara, is pacing around the living room as she talks to Aunt Martha, who is in her corner at Down Stage Right, lying on her stomach on a chiropractor table talking on her cell phone while the **CHIROPRACTOR,** *a nice looking man in his mid-thirties, is manipulating her.*

AUNT MARTHA. A lot of people become allergic to peanuts. It's very common. You can eat them for years and years and suddenly overnight they turn on you.

SARA. I thought he was a goner this time. His throat closed up completely. The paramedics said peanuts can actually be more fatal than tuna fish.

AUNT MARTHA. Did you give him mouth to mouth again?

SARA. Yes, I did.

AUNT MARTHA. See. Something good comes from everything. Oh, Sara. It's wonderful to see you're so concerned for a man. I'll bet if you exhibited these feelings before not so many of your male clients would have gone to jail.

SARA. Most of my male clients go to jail because they're guilty. They hire me to get them a lighter sentence, which unfortunately I do. My concern for Brandon was not because he's a man but because he's a human being, who through no fault of his own, was clobbered over the head and almost choked to death twice. You've got to stop this absurdity, Aunt Martha. He's confused enough and frankly at this point so am I.

AUNT MARTHA. You confused? That's the most encouraging thing I've heard. What if I take the two of you out for dinner and right after the entree explain to him what I've done? Then we'll all have a big laugh and maybe some tiramisu for dessert and we'll talk about buying out Heather.

(Brandon starts to moan)

SARA. I need to go, Aunt Martha. Brandon is moaning and I'm migraining and you're responsible for both.

(She hangs up. LIGHTS OUT on Aunt Martha)

BRANDON. Oh, wow, my chest is killing me. Did I get pumped again?

SARA. You did.

BRANDON. And mouth to mouth? I got that too, right?

SARA. You did.

BRANDON. I'm really worried. I'm starting to like that. Peanut butter. Go figure. My stomach feels like it's been scoured out with steel wool.

SARA. I'm sure a little oatmeal will fix it right up. When I stopped off for the peanut butter and jelly yesterday I also bought some instant oatmeal. It's amazing stuff. You just add water and zap it in the microwave for one minute which, by certain standards I believe is considered cooking. I also picked up a bread for the sandwiches and a lettuce. The lettuce was to more or less balance out my shopping cart. I thought it needed something green.

BRANDON. The check out person must have been very impressed.

SARA. He was. I'll get the oatmeal. You'd better call Heather. Your cell was ringing in your jacket most of the night.

BRANDON. Thanks. I'll get right on it. Listen, I'm sorry about last night and unloading my marriage hang-ups on you. I was being a total jerk.

SARA. That's okay. I wasn't exactly a specimen of delight myself.

BRANDON. I guess we were just two upset people. I was upset about my marriage concerns and you were upset because I upset you. Anyway, I think all I needed was a good rest because I absolutely don't feel apprehensive about the marriage anymore.

SARA. *(A bit disappointed)* No?

BRANDON. No. You were right. I need to think happiness. I need to think, joy, romance and love. I plan to start the very minute I leave here. I wouldn't be at all surprised if it does the trick.

SARA. Hmmm! I'll get your oatmeal. Call Heather.

(She EXITS to kitchen)

BRANDON. Right. Besides, It's gone too far. She has her silver pattern picked out. Her linens, her crystal. Just because I'm a little apprehensive doesn't mean it's not going to work out and that Heather and I won't live happily ever after, right?

SARA (O.S.) What?

BRANDON. Nothing.

(He goes to his jacket and takes out his cell phone. A card drops to the floor. He picks it up and reads it aloud)

Noogie Malloy Enterprises?

(He shrugs his shoulders, puts the card back in his jacket and tries to dial on the cell phone)

Damn.

(Calling to Sara in the kitchen)

My cell phone is dead. Mind if I use your phone?

SARA (O.S.) Please, go right ahead.

(Brandon goes to Sara's desk and picks up her phone and begins dialing. He looks around the room as he waits for the phone to connect. LIGHTS UP Down Stage Left on Heather as she answers)

HEATHER. Hello.

BRANDON. Heather. It's Brandon. Don't hang up. I can

explain about last night. You know how allergic I am to tuna fish? Well, I'm also allergic to peanuts.

HEATHER. Do you realize I spent a whole day yesterday preparing some stupid French dish for you I can't even pronounce?

BRANDON. I'll have it tonight.

HEATHER. Don't bother. It's in the garbage. Besides, tonight we're going to my friend Wendy's studio remember? She's showing her new paintings and it's important we be there. God, Brandon, you really disappoint me sometimes. I had to spend the entire evening talking to my parents all by myself. Just where are you anyway?

BRANDON. I'm uh...I'm at my apartment. Yes, that's where I am.

HEATHER. Really? Then why didn't you answer the phone when I called?

BRANDON. Well, I uh...

HEATHER. You're at that Sara's apartment, aren't you?

BRANDON. Well, uh, yes. You see it seems I had to have more pumping again last night and some mouth to mouth, which was actually terrific. I mean it was terrific because it saved my life, but I think there was a little too much pumping because this morning I woke up sore as hell and uh, listen, I'm not sure this is coming out right, especially this pumping business. Can I start all over?

(Heather hangs up. LIGHTS OUT on her area)

BRANDON *(CONTINUED)* Heather! Heather!

(He hangs up the phone and shakes his head)

Why am I so dumb?

(He then notices the stack of business cards Noogie left on Sara's desk. He picks one up and reads it curiously)

Noogie Malloy Enterprises?

(Calls off to Sara)

Who is Noogie Malloy?

SARA. *(ENTERING with a tray that contains a bowl of oatmeal, a glass of water, eating utensils and a napkin)* What?

BRANDON. I said, who is Noogie Malloy?

(Sara drops the tray to the ground)

BRANDON *(CONTINUED)* Are you okay?

SARA. *(Nodding her head, obviously shaken)* I'm fine. I'm fine.

(She gets down on her knees to clean up. Brandon gets down with her)

BRANDON. Let me help you clean this up.

SARA. No. No please. No problem. I'll take care of it.

(She begins cleaning up with the napkin)

Did you call Heather?

BRANDON. Yes. She hung up on me. You're right. I've got to stop lying. But I did it so she wouldn't think anything funny was going on between us. Sometimes, in certain situations, you need to lie.

SARA. I couldn't agree with you more.

BRANDON. Anyway, I'll just pick up more roses.

SARA. Yes. Maybe this time try two dozen.

(They are now looking at one another, speaking a little slower)

BRANDON. Good advice. I'm sure I'll have it all straightened out by tonight. We're going to an art exhibit. I don't really like the artist, but she's a friend of Heather's. She's into penises.

SARA. Heather or the artist?

BRANDON. The artist. That's all she paints, penises. All sizes, shapes and colors and larger than life. I hate her work. I always leave feeling very inadequate.

(They look at one another for a beat. Their lips seem much too close)

BRANDON *(CONTINUED)* You smell very nice.

SARA. That's the oatmeal. It has maple in it.

(Sara backs away and finishes cleaning)

Maybe you should get over to Heather with the roses as soon as possible. Quite frankly, if my fiancée woke up two nights in a row in a strange woman's apartment, I'd be a little upset too.

(She starts to rise with the tray and dishes)

BRANDON. I'll call her from my office. Now tell me, who Noogie Malloy is.

(Sara drops the tray and dishes again)

BRANDON *(CONTINUED)* Are you all right?

SARA. No. Yes. I'm fine.

(They both start cleaning up again)

You might be better off grabbing something on the way to your office. My body is apparently rebelling from anything kitchen-related.

BRANDON. Sure. But now I'm curious. Who is this Noogie Malloy? You have a bunch of his cards on your desk and I found one in my pocket.

SARA. You did? Yes, I remember you saying that. Noogie Malloy. Isn't that a coincidence? You have Noogie's card and I have a bunch of Noogie's cards.

BRANDON. Yes. Who is he?

SARA. Noogie Malloy? Well, he's a…a cousin.

BRANDON. A cousin.

SARA. Right. A distant one. A very distant one who started a business.

BRANDON. So what was his card doing in my jacket pocket?

SARA. What was it doing in your jacket pocket?

BRANDON. Are you having trouble understanding me? You keep repeating everything.

SARA. Yes, I do keep repeating everything, don't I? What was Noogie's card doing in your pocket? Well, I'm sure it's easy to explain. Uh, where did you say your office was?

BRANDON. Downtown.

SARA. Well, then that explains it.

BRANDON. Explains what?

SARA. How you got his card. That's his area. That's where he passes out his cards. People in New York are always passing out things. I once got a flyer walking down 5th Avenue from this company that was selling six hundred dollar men's suits for forty-nine-fifty. What a bargain. Imagine. If I was a guy and bought three suits I could have saved fifteen hundred dollars. I was sick about it for weeks.

BRANDON. I don't remember anyone passing out any card to me.

SARA. No? Well, Noogie obviously must have given it to you during your blackout period when you were probably walking around in a fog or something.

BRANDON. I guess it is possible.

SARA. It's the only explanation that makes sense, I hope... I mean, I think.

BRANDON. What does he do?

(Sara has everything on the tray. They rise)

SARA. Who?

BRANDON. Your cousin. It doesn't say what he does on his card.

SARA. Well, uh, things.

BRANDON. Like?

SARA. Like things. He's kind of a jack of all trades, but between you and me, I wouldn't use him.

BRANDON. No?

SARA. He's not that good. He'll just give you one big headache after another. If I were you, I'd just tear up his card.

(Sara places the tray on the desk and then takes the cards Noogie left her)

In fact, I'm going to tear up mine right now.

(She begins tearing up Noogie's cards)

See. Look, I'm tearing them up. All of them. He's really the black sheep of the family. I mean, I never have him over for dinner or anything. Let me tear up yours? Why carry it around if you're never going to use him?

(The PHONE RINGS)

Excuse me.

(Picks up phone)

Yes!

(LIGHTS UP on Aunt Martha's corner. She is on her cell phone still being manipulated by the Chiropractor)

AUNT MARTHA. Is he still there?

SARA. What? Oh, hello, Aunt Martha? What? Cousin Noogie? I was just talking about him?

AUNT MARTHA. What about cousin Noogie? He's not a cousin.

SARA. Oh, no.

BRANDON & AUNT MARTHA. What happened?

SARA. *(To Brandon)* Oh, it's just awful. Cousin Noogie. He was walking down the street…

BRANDON & AUNT MARTHA. And?

SARA. And an air conditioning unit fell out of the window and killed him.

BRANDON & AUNT MARTHA. No?

SARA. *(To Brandon)* See, I told you those things happen.

AUNT MARTHA. Oh, the poor man. And to think I put him on a retainer.

SARA. *(To Brandon)* It's too bad. You would have liked him. He did terrible work, but he's a hoot at parties.

(On phone)

So long, Aunt Martha. See you at the funeral.

(She hangs up)

BRANDON. I'm terribly sorry.

SARA. About what?

BRANDON. Your cousin Noogie.

SARA. Oh, Noogie. Right. Well, I'm very fortunate. I have a lot of other cousins. Anyway, that solves that issue, doesn't it? Now, you need to get to work and I have this case that's going to trial.

BRANDON. Yes, well, once again, thanks for everything you've done.

SARA. My pleasure.

BRANDON. Was it?

SARA. Yes. Now and then it really was. Goodbye, Brandon and good luck.

(She picks up the tray to bring to the kitchen)

BRANDON. Goodbye, Sara.

(Brandon takes a few steps towards the door and then stop and turns to Sara)

I need to do one more thing.

SARA. What?

BRANDON. This.

(He goes to her and gives her a long kiss on the lips. She drops the tray to the ground)

BRANDON *(CONTINUED)* Thank goodness. I knew it wasn't the paramedics.

(He takes his briefcase and EXITS. Sara stands at the door, stunned. She closes the door and touches her lips for a moment in confusion. She then puts all the dropped dishes back on the tray, still moved by the kiss. THE PHONE RINGS. She picks it up)

SARA. Oh, God, Aunt Martha. He kissed me.

*(LIGHTS UP on **HEATHER**)*

HEATHER. He what?

SARA. *(Not realizing it isn't Aunt Martha)* And I think I liked it.

HEATHER. Is this Sara Hastings?

SARA. Uh, Yes.

HEATHER. This is Heather Boyd, Brandon Cates' fiancée.

SARA. *(Horrified)* It is? Well, how nice of you to call. How did you get my number?

HEATHER. You're in the book.

SARA. Oh, yes. Yes, I am. How nice of you to call. I think I said that.

HEATHER. I think we need to talk.

SARA. Oh. Oh, yes. Absolutely.

(A second line RINGS)

Could you hold please. My other line is ringing.

(Sara switches to the other line. LIGHTS UP on Aunt Martha in the other corner still being manipulated by the chiropractor)

AUNT MARTHA. Sara, what's wrong with you? I called up Noogie and he's healthy as a horse.

SARA. Aunt Martha. I think we're in trouble. Brandon's fiancée is on the other line and she wants to talk. I don't know what to do.

AUNT MARTHA. Oh. Well, don't worry. I'm sure I'll come up with something.

(Aunt Martha hangs up. LIGHTS OUT on her)

SARA. Right. *(Aloud to herself)* Right? Did I say right?

(On the phone)

Aunt Martha! Aunt Martha! What the hell am I doing?

(She switches to the other line)

SARA *(CONTINUED)* Hello, Heather?

HEATHER. Yes.

SARA. You were saying…you think we need to talk?

HEATHER. Better yet. I think we need to meet, face to face.

SARA. Meet? Yes. Well, uh, maybe you can come up here for lunch. I have a lettuce in the fridge that I have no idea what to do with.

(A confused expression takes over both their faces)

SLOW FADE

End of Act II, Scene 1

Scene 2

TIME: Early afternoon. Sara is on the phone. Aunt Martha is LIT in her corner area. She is on her head set, wearing leotards and eating yogurt out of a container.

AUNT MARTHA. Let me have that again. You invited Heather up to your apartment?

SARA. We are ruining this poor girl's life and it isn't fair. I made up my mind that when she gets here I'm going to tell her everything.

AUNT MARTHA. Really? How much of everything?

SARA. The works. That I have an aunt that's a total whacko.

AUNT MARTHA. You know, Sara, I really resent the word whacko. Can't you use something a little more dignified like "odd" or "eccentric"? Anyway, all I know is that this is the most involved you've ever been with a man and I am very encouraged.

SARA. And I am very stressed. I've got a trial coming up and I have no idea how I'm ever going to get through it. Anyway, right now all I want from you is the promise that these shenanigans are all over and that you will never, ever bother Brandon again.

AUNT MARTHA. Oh, Sara, I just love the fact that you're so concerned about him.

SARA. I am not.

AUNT MARTHA. You are so.

SARA. I am not.

AUNT MARTHA. You are so.

SARA. Who cares?

AUNT MARTHA. You do. Anyway, I can't make any promises because the wheels of progress are already in motion.

SARA. What does that mean?

AUNT MARTHA. Brandon should be arriving about now.

SARA. No, no. Not again.

AUNT MARTHA. Please, Sara. I've gone through a lot of trouble to get you two this far. Try and help the effort.

(DOORBELL)

SARA. Oh, God. That's either Noogie with Brandon or Heather with a gun.

AUNT MARTHA. Just rise to the occasion darling. I know you can do it.

(Sara hangs up. Aunt Martha's corner goes DARK. An impatient DOORBELL RINGS again. Sara goes to the door and opens it. To her surprise it's Brandon standing there. She is obviously happy to see him, especially standing)

SARA. Brandon. You're conscious. I'm so happy.

BRANDON. Are you really?

SARA. Of course I am. Look how I'm smiling.

BRANDON. I have a little gift for you.

SARA. Roses?

BRANDON. Not exactly.

(He then reaches over and pulls the dolly into the middle of the room with an unconscious Noogie strapped to it. Noogie is clutching Brandon's briefcase)

SARA. Noogie!

BRANDON. Cousin Noogie, remember? Apparently the air conditioner that fell on his head didn't kill him.

(Brandon takes the briefcase from Noogie's hands, puts it on an end table and then unstraps Noogie who falls to the floor.)

I was on my way to the office. I got in the elevator and saw your pal here. He got in and moved right behind me which seemed a little suspicious and suddenly it all came clear to me. I had seen him twice before. Both times when I got in the elevator. That's when everything would go black and I'd wake up here. And just in the few seconds that I was putting it all together, in the corner of my eye I saw him lift his arm with a little metal object in his hand and I turned around and decked him.

SARA. You did. I'm so impressed.

BRANDON. I wasn't trying to impress you. I was trying to protect my head. You know what was really upsetting? Every time I got in that elevator it was always packed with people and no one ever did anything to help me. What the hell is wrong with this city? Where's their sense of responsibility? Where's their concern for their fellow citizen? Where's their grasp of civic duty?

SARA. It's terrible isn't it? I think one of us should write a letter to the *New York Times*.

BRANDON. Anyway, I went through his pockets and found these cards of his.

(Reaches into his pocket and pulls out a handful of Noogie's cards and hands them to Sara)

Noogie Malloy Enterprises. I knew just where to bring him.

SARA. *(Avoids taking the cards)* Brandon, I want you to know I had nothing to do with this. I just found out a few seconds ago my Aunt Martha was planning to get you bonked again. So help me, I would have called to warn you had I known sooner.

BRANDON. Your aunt? She's behind this?

SARA. She had this crazy scheme to marry us off.

BRANDON. I'm engaged.

SARA. She felt it could still work out.

BRANDON. Your aunt. Damn, I knew she was a loon.

SARA. Look, Brandon, you have the right to press charges, to haul us both in, but I'm asking you not to. My aunt is a well meaning, sweet, little old maniac and I promise to get her under control one way or another. God, Brandon, I'm so sorry.

(She reaches and strokes the top of his head)

And oh, your poor head. I'm just so...so upset by all this. I feel like I'm going to cry.

BRANDON. No, wait. Don't cry. Please, don't cry. I'm really not very good with women that cry.

SARA. *(Weakly)* You're not?

BRANDON. Not at all.

SARA. I've never felt so awful.

(Sara begins to sniffle. Brandon goes to her and holds her to comfort her)

BRANDON. Please, don't. I can deal with anything but a woman crying.

(He holds her a bit longer than he should. It's almost too comfortable)

SARA. This is so unlike me. I never get emotional. I never cry.

BRANDON. Well, maybe it's good to do it once in a while. I read where crying does have some beneficial function.

SARA. It smudges your makeup.

BRANDON. Yes, but you don't wear any make up.

SARA. You noticed?

BRANDON. I noticed a lot of things about you, Sarah. You're a very special girl.

SARA. I just hate that word.

BRANDON. Okay, how about attractive?

SARA. That's a little better.

BRANDON. Warm.

SARA. Not bad.

BRANDON. Soft.

SARA. That's good too.

BRANDON. Very soft, extremely soft…

(They are both very comfortable in each others arms. There are a few beats of contented silence)

SARA. Brandon?

BRANDON. What?

SARA. This conversation is making me very nervous.

BRANDON. Why?

SARA. Because we're not talking.

(She breaks away)

This isn't right. This is not what we should be doing. There are too many other things to deal with.

BRANDON. Like what?

SARA. Like Noogie, who's not really my cousin, and my aunt who unfortunately really is my aunt, and your fiancée Heather, who is about to go postal.

BRANDON. Why?

(The DOORBELL RINGS)

SARA. Well, I believe you're about to find out right now.

(Sara goes to the door and opens it. It's Heather. They both seem surprised by each others appearance. Heather is of course dressed in brown)

HEATHER. Hello.

SARA. Heather?

HEATHER. Yes. Sara?

(Brandon, in disbelief, sits on the sofa trying to make himself very small. Not waiting to be invited, Heather ENTERS the room)

SARA. Yes. Please come in.

(Sara closes the door. Heather spots Brandon's briefcase and points at it)

HEATHER. That's the briefcase case I bought Brandon.

SARA. You have fabulous taste.

HEATHER. *(Pointing. Upset)* And that's Brandon.

BRANDON. Where? Oh, yes. So it is. I mean, I am. It's me.

HEATHER. You're still here?

BRANDON. *(Desperate. Rising)* Yes, but uh, I can explain everything, right, Sara?

SARA. *(Calmly)* We can only hope. By the way, Heather, I love that color on you.

BLACK OUT

End of Act II, Scene 2

Scene 3

TIME: About twenty minutes later. Noogie is still on the floor unconscious. Heather is sitting on the sofa. Brandon sits on the sofa's arm. Sara is standing.

HEATHER. And that's it. A screwball aunt that wants to fix up her unmarried niece.

SARA. That's it. Nothing more. At no time was there ever anything between Brandon and myself that you need to be at all worried about. Right, Brandon?

BRANDON. Oh, uh, yeah...I mean no, nothing to worry about.

HEATHER. Well, yes, I see that now. But you can understand my concern. Brandon was a confirmed bachelor when we met and to be honest, even though we are getting married, every now and then I got the feeling that he might be having a case of buyers remorse.

SARA. Oh, no. You aren't are you, Brandon?

BRANDON. Oh, uh, yeah, I mean, no. No remorse. Not at all.

HEATHER. Good, because I've got my heart set on being your wife, Brandon and I wouldn't want anything to get in the way of that. Anyway, it's quite clear to me that Aunt Martha needs to be dealt with.

SARA. I agree wholeheartedly.

HEATHER. It's very possible that long after Brandon and I have married, she could still be bonking him on the head and dragging him off to you.

SARA. I know, but I'm sure with therapy and heavy duty medication, we can keep her under control.

HEATHER. I wish we could believe that.

BRANDON. Why can't we?

HEATHER. I'm not sure Aunt Martha is sane enough to trust. I have a psycho uncle who lives in fear of being abducted by aliens from another planet. Every night he sleeps under tin foil so their surveillance cameras

won't detect him. They say if he just took his pre-
scribed medicine he could live a normal life. But he
won't because he doesn't want to take the chance of
waking up one morning on Mars. I don't think your
Aunt Martha is going to back off until...

SARA. Yes?

HEATHER. Until you are safely married. That's why I think
the only solution is that you need to get married and I
believe Brandon and I can help you along with that. Now
Brandon, how about Tim Larsen? He's not that good
looking, but I still think they'd make a nice couple.

BRANDON. He's at least a full foot shorter than her.

HEATHER. He slouches. After they marry she can take him
to an orthopedist. In fact, that could be our wedding
gift to them. A gift certificate for six visits.

BRANDON. Not Tim Larsen.

HEATHER. Okay. Then how about Bert Ridgley?

BRANDON. He's the most boring man I know.

HEATHER. Well, yes, we think so, but that doesn't mean they
won't hit it off. There are a number of boring couples
who adore each other. Oh, I'm so sorry, Sara. I hope
that didn't sound like I was insinuating that you were
boring?

SARA. I think it did.

HEATHER. I apologize. I truly didn't mean it that way.

BRANDON. Bert Ridgley is not the guy for Sara.

HEATHER. No?

BRANDON. No.

HEATHER. Okay. Then what about Jonathan Clay?

BRANDON. The taxidermist? Oh, my God. He reeks from
formaldehyde. Besides, he's not her type either.

HEATHER. Really, Brandon, don't you think we should let
Sara decide that for herself?

BRANDON. Why waste her time? Look, I've spent two nights
with her. I should know something about the kind of
guy she needs. That didn't come out right, did it?

HEATHER. No it did not. Look, I don't mean to sound unsympathetic, but who's best interests are you looking out for, hers or mine?

SARA. That's true, Brandon. You sound much too concerned about me.

BRANDON. I'm sorry.

SARA. That's okay. Just be aware of it next time. I'm sure these past few days have been very upsetting for Heather.

HEATHER. They certainly have. And the sooner Sara has someone, the sooner you'll stop getting bonked on the head. I do not want to marry a vegetable. The only other solution is to simply get a court order and confine Aunt Martha to an institution of some sort.

(*Noogie starts to come to. He gets up rubbing his chin*)

NOOGIE. Oh, wow. That was good. And I've been taken out by the best.

(*To Brandon*)

It was you, right?

BRANDON. Yeah.

NOOGIE. Your aunt is okay, Sara. She picked out a very healthy one for you.

(*To Heather*)

Did we meet?

HEATHER. I don't believe I've had the pleasure.

NOOGIE. Then I'll give it to you. I'm Noogie Malloy. Here's my card.

(*Goes through pockets*)

They're gone.

BRANDON. I took them.

NOOGIE. Oh, good. Give one to her. I've got hundreds more at home. Well, it looks like you kids have a lot to discuss and I've got a busy day ahead of me so I'll be going.

BRANDON. No, you won't. You'll stay right here till we get a few things settled.

NOOGIE. *(Looks at watch)* It's after one. I haven't had my lunch yet.

BRANDON. How do you feel about prison food?

NOOGIE. *(Indicating Sara)* Talk to my lawyer.

SARA. I'm not taking the case. Look, Noogie. This head bonking has got to stop.

NOOGIE. Hey, it's not my idea. I'm just the messenger. Your aunt is sending the messages. Besides, if she didn't hire me she would have just gotten someone else. Believe it or not, I'm in a very competitive business. There are tons of women out there looking for Mr. Right. Now what about lunch? Anything in the kitchen?

SARA. Surprise yourself.

NOOGIE. Thanks.

(Rubs chin)

Boy, what a smack. I'm very impressed.

(He EXITS to kitchen)

HEATHER. Okay, so Tim, Bert, and Jonathan are out. What about a dating service? We'll take a photo of Sara and have it air brushed. She's bound to get someone.

SARA. Look, I don't need to be air brushed or fixed up. Trust me, if I make up my mind to land someone, I'll land him. I'm not married because I choose not to be and maybe it's time I let my aunt know the reasons. Excuse me.

(Picks up phone and begins dialing. Then to Heather)

You may not want to hear this.

HEATHER. Of course I do.

SARA. Good.

(LIGHTS UP on Aunt Martha Down Stage Right. She is sitting on a raised platform doing yoga. Her legs are crossed in the lotus position)

AUNT MARTHA. Ooooohm! Ooooohm!

(The PHONE RINGS. She puts on her head set and continues to stay in the lotus position)

Martha here.

SARA. Aunt Martha. It's Sara.

AUNT MARTHA. Sara, dear. How's it going? I'm keeping my fingers crossed. Oooohm! Ooooohm!

SARA. Aunt Martha, I obviously haven't made it clear why I don't want a man in my life so let me try to do it now with a little visualization.

BRANDON. Oh oh.

(During the following Sara paces the floor with the phone in her hand)

SARA. Picture this. I wake up one morning and my world is different because now there's a man in my life. He's not in my bed, because it's Sunday morning and he's playing golf with the boys. I walk into the bathroom and what do I find?

AUNT MARTHA. I give up.

SARA. The toilet seat is up, the hot water is gone, his smelly old clothes and underwear that have been lying on the floor for the last five days are still there and worse than that he's used my tooth brush.

HEATHER. Gross.

SARA. Next, I go to the kitchen, but first I need to pass through a once beautiful living room, which is now taken over by his bright green Lazy-Boy lounge chair and his wall to wall entertainment center with the wide screen television which has made the room so incredibly ugly that I keep my eyes closed every time I pass through it.

HEATHER. *(To Brandon)* You have both those things.

BRANDON. Yeah, but my Lazy-Boy is orange.

SARA. I open the fridge to be confronted by another nightmare. It's totally filled with cans of Budweiser, because when his unruly friends come over to watch football on Monday night, basketball on Saturday afternoon and play all night poker on Thursdays, they need their beer.

BRANDON. *(To Heather)* I thought about it and I'm stopping the Monday night football.

SARA. Then along comes pregnancy and with it morning sickness and puking my brains out and with my luck it's twins, Herman and Milton, named after his two favorite uncles. And now for the next two years, my days are filled with trying to get that putrid mashed baby food down their throats which somehow they keep spitting back up on me.

HEATHER & AUNT MARTHA. Yuk!

SARA. And every where I walk are bags filled with disposable diapers that reek of baby urine and baby poop because while Mr. Right found time to make those babies, he just can't find the time to throw what *they make* in the garbage. The stench can actually lift a house off its foundation.

HEATHER. *(To Brandon)* She's quite graphic, isn't she?

SARA. And as my life continues being filled up with runny noses and soiled laundry and sleepless nights, I discover another kid is on the way and here comes another three more months of puking my guts up.

HEATHER. We were planning to have a big family weren't we?

BRANDON. Well, yeah. You said you wanted one, remember?

(Sara walks towards Heather standing practically toe to toe with her during the following)

SARA. And the years go by with more baby vomit and more smelly everything and as the kids get bigger and bigger my space becomes smaller and smaller because now it's filled up with constant trips to the pediatrician and the orthodontist and math tutors and school counseling and never-ending-screaming at those brats to stop fighting with each other and do their goddamn homework.

AUNT MARTHA. Honey, should I come over there with some Valium?

SARA. And the years continue to pass and the wrinkles on my face continue to multiply and my waist begins to expand because with taking care of all those kids I've had no time to go to the gym. And where is the jerk I married now?

HEATHER. Where?

SARA. *(To Heather while still on the phone)* He's off with a new toupee and some young twenty-year old tramp who is going to help him find his lost youth, while I just become more and more suicidal, because at the ripe old age of forty-five, I'm finally beginning to realize that life has screwed *me* royally.

(Back at Aunt Martha)

Well, the hell with that, Aunt Martha. That's not the way I'm going to end up because, no man, dead or alive, is worth my giving up my wonderful, uncomplicated, beautiful single life for. So please keep that in mind the next time you get any more bright ideas to fix me up. Take care and let's have lunch one day.

(She slams the phone down. LIGHTS OUT on a speechless Aunt Martha. **SARA** *looks* **HEATHER** *right in the eye)*

How was that?

HEATHER. Oh, my God. Oh, my God. It was…It was…I think I'm going to be sick.

(Heather puts her hand over her mouth as if she's about to puke and RUNS OUT the door)

BRANDON. *(Starts to go after her)* Heather!

(To Sara)

Look what you've done. You've scared the hell out of her.

SARA. I know. She's obviously very sensitive. Anyway, you have to admit she had it coming. Trying to fix me up with Jonathan the taxidermist was way over the line. You're not angry are you?

BRANDON. Right now, I don't know what I am. I'd better go after her before she throws herself in front of a bus.

(He grabs his briefcase and EXITS)

SARA. *(Aloud to herself)* He's angry. Maybe I shouldn't have done it. Why did I do it? It was very small of me.

(Noogie comes out of the kitchen eating a peanut butter sandwich and she now addresses him)

SARA *(CONTINUED)* I should just let them get married, right? Even though they're absolutely wrong for each other. I'm so confused. Did I scare her away to get even or do I really like the guy? You tell me?

NOOGIE. Can't help you. I missed the conversation. Anyway, I made peanut butter and jelly sandwiches. I haven't had one of these since I was a kid. They're delicious. This is my second one. You really should have milk with these. Oh. Oooooh. Oooooooh.

(He begins choking and grabs at his neck)

SARA. What?

NOOGIE. I don't know. My throat. It's clogging up. I can't breathe.

SARA. Why am I not surprised?

(She picks up phone and dials)

Operator. I need a paramedic.

(Looks at Noogie who is holding his throat and gasping for air. His knees are starting to buckle)

Pick out a nice soft place on the floor, Noogie. Just don't count on me for mouth to mouth.

(Noogie topples over)

BLACK OUT

End of Act II, Scene 3

Scene 4

TIME: *Later that night. Sara is on the phone*

SARA Look Lou, I'm just not going to be ready to go to court. If I'm to do a half way decent job, I need an extension. Yes, I know you hate the client and so do I, but it's our duty to give him the best defense we can and right now I'm not in any position or mood to do that…Well, other things came up, like tuna fish and peanut butter. I know it's not a good combination but that's the problem. Just get the extension, Lou. Thanks.

(Hangs up)

I'm not myself. There's no question about it, I'm not myself.

(The DOORBELL RINGS)

SARA *(CONTINUED)* Which could be an improvement.

(She opens the door. It's Brandon)

Brandon?

BRANDON. *(He ENTERS)* Look, this afternoon I left a bit irritated.

(Sara closes the door)

SARA. You had every right to be. I was wrong in what I did and if you'd like, I'll call Heather and apologize. Actually, I can see why you were attracted to her. She's quite pretty. Eventually I'll bet she'll get into other colors besides brown.

BRANDON. Maybe.

SARA. I wouldn't be at all surprised if your marriage worked out. Most marriages don't, you know. Those are the statistics. As a friend, I thought I should pass along that information because, as they say, knowledge is power, but frankly I don't think marriage should be about power as much as it should be about other things, which I haven't had time to think about yet because of my busy work schedule, but once I get caught up with whatever it is I have to get caught up with, I'll get on that right away and then maybe the two of us can figure out why I'm so stupidly babbling on like this.

BRANDON. How about, because you like me?

SARA. Yes, of course. I mean, no. I mean…

BRANDON. Heather broke our engagement.

SARA. *(Elated)* She did?

(Catching herself. Less jubilant)

Well, what did I tell you? That visualization drivel you came up with could frighten the hell out of anyone. I hope you didn't rent your tuxedo yet.

BRANDON. She really wasn't ready for marriage with me anymore than I was with her. We both were settling and we let it go too far. Anyway, better to be disappointed today rather than regretful tomorrow.

SARA. I had a fortune cookie with that same message.

BRANDON. Now I need to address something else. I did the visualization bit again right before I came over. My bathroom filled with bras and panties, a life in suburbia with six kids and tons of baby vomit and so on and so on.

SARA. And?

BRANDON. And when it was your bras and panties and our six kids, I felt nothing but happiness, joy, romance and love. It was wonderful.

SARA. It was? Oh, damn it, Brandon, I don't know if this is appropriate? You're barely unengaged. Shouldn't there be a bereavement period?

BRANDON. There was. Heather broke up with me over two hours ago.

SARA. Oh, well, that's different. So then what you're saying is that…

BRANDON. I want to bring my stadium size TV and my orange Lazy-Boy lounge chair here.

SARA. No. No, you can't.

BRANDON. Why not?

SARA. Because I like my life. I like my freedom, I like my bathroom, I like my space...

(Brandon takes her in his arms and kisses her)

How soon can we get that ugly chair up here?

(They kiss again. The DOORBELL RINGS. Sara and Brandon give each other a curious look)

Hold that thought.

(Sara opens the door. It's Noogie)

Oh, no.

NOOGIE. *(WHEELING in the unconscious Chiropractor on his dolly)*

Hi, kid. It's from your aunt. She said she's disappointed things didn't work out with Brandon so she's sending you the Chiropractor.

SARA. I see.

(As Noogie goes about unloading the Chiropractor, Sara returns to Brandon and puts her arms around him)

SARA *(CONTINUED) (Deep breath)* Maybe it's possible Aunt Martha knows what she's doing. Now where were we?

BRANDON. Maybe this will remind you.

(They kiss as the lights...)

SLOW FADE

THE END

PROPS

ACT I

Scene 1
Deli wrapped tuna sandwich
Hand weights
Head set for Aunt Martha
Briefcase for Brandon
Dolly – to support a man
Delivery receipt
Pen
Glass of water
Man's wallet
Theater tickets in envelope

Scene 2
Blanket
Stationary bike
Head set for Aunt Martha
Glass of water
Cell phone
Telephone on small table for Heather
Tray with oatmeal. Tea, spoon, napkins

Scene 3
Peanut butter and jelly sandwich
Briefcase
Dolly
Head set for Aunt Martha
Guitar
Stool
Delivery receipt
Small stack of business cards *(20)*

ACT II

Scene 1
Blanket
Chiropractor table
Cell phone
Business card
Telephone on small table for Heather
Tray with bowl of oatmeal, glass of water, napkin and utensils

Scene 2
Yogurt
Spoon
Headset for Aunt Martha
Dolly
Briefcase
Business cards *(20)*

Scene 3
Peanut Butter sandwich
Headset for Aunt Martha

Scene 4
Dolly

COSTUMES

ACT I

Scene 1
Sara – Jeans and sweatshirt
Aunt Martha – Warm up suit
Noogie – Black suit, white shirt, black tie
Brandon – Suit, shirt, tie and watch

Scene 2
Sara – slacks, sweater
Aunt Martha – A different athletic outfit
Brandon – Same as in Scene 1
Heather – Brown dress, brown apron

Scene 3
Sara – Same as Scene 2
Aunt Martha – Same as in Scene 2
Noogie – Same black suit, white shirt, black tie
Brandon – A different suit, shirt, tie

ACT II

Scene 1
Sara – Skirt and sweater, necklace
Brandon – Same as in Act I, Scene 3
Aunt Martha – Long sleeve tee shirt and yoga pants
Chiropractor – White pants, white tee shirt
Heather – A different brown dress

Scene 2
Sara – Same as scene 1
Aunt Martha – A long sweater over her yoga pants
Noogie – Same black suit, white shirt, black tie
Brandon – Sport jacket, slacks, shirt tie
Heather – Same as scene 1

Scene 3
Sara - Same as scene 1
Brandon - Same as scene 2
Noogie – Same black suit, white shirt, black tie
Chiropractor – Same white slacks and white tee shirt

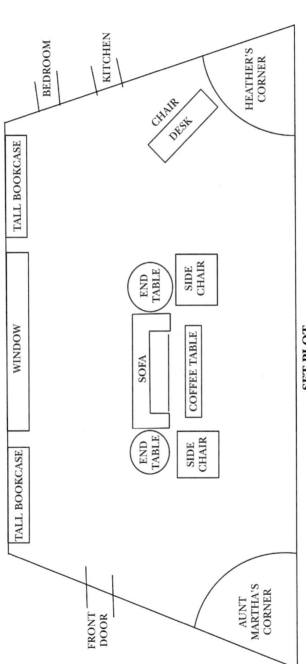

SET PLOT

Also by
Sam Bobrick...

Annoyance
Are You Sure?
Baggage
The Crazy Time
Death in England
Flemming (An American Thriller)
Hamlet II (Better Than the Original)
Last Chance Romance
Murder at the Howard Johnson's
New York Water
No Hard Feelings
Norman, Is That You?
The Outrageous Adventures of
Sheldon and Mrs. Levine
Passengers
Remember Me?
Splitting Issues
The Stanway Case
Wally's Cafe
Weekend Comedy

Please visit our website **samuelfrench.com** for complete
descriptions and licensing information

OTHER TITLES AVAILABLE FROM SAMUEL FRENCH

MAURITIUS
Theresa Rebeck

Comedy / 3m, 2f / Interior

Stamp collecting is far more risky than you think. After their mother's death, two estranged half-sisters discover a book of rare stamps that may include the crown jewel for collectors. One sister tries to collect on the windfall, while the other resists for sentimental reasons. In this gripping tale, a seemingly simple sale becomes dangerous when three seedy, high-stakes collectors enter the sisters' world, willing to do anything to claim the rare find as their own.

"(Theresa Rebeck's) belated Broadway bow, the only original play by a woman to have its debut on Broadway this fall."
- Robert Simonson, *New York Times*

"*Mauritius* caters efficiently to a hunger that Broadway hasn't been gratifying in recent years. That's the corkscrew-twist drama of suspense… she has strewn her script with a multitude of mysteries."
- Ben Brantley, *New York Times*

"Theresa Rebeck is a slick playwright… Her scenes have a crisp shape, her dialogue pops, her characters swagger through an array of showy emotion, and she knows how to give a plot a cunning twist."
- John Lahr, *The New Yorker*

OTHER TITLES AVAILABLE FROM SAMUEL FRENCH

EVIL DEAD: THE MUSICAL
Book & Lyrics By George Reinblatt
Music By Frank Cipolla/Christopher Bond/Melissa Morris/
George Reinblatt

Musical Comedy / 6m, 4f / Unit set

Based on Sam Raimi's 80s cult classic films, *Evil Dead* tells the tale of 5 college kids who travel to a cabin in the woods and accidentally unleash an evil force. And although it may sound like a horror, its not! The songs are hilariously campy and the show is bursting with more farce than a Monty Python skit. *Evil Dead: The Musical* unearths the old familiar story: boy and friends take a weekend getaway at abandoned cabin, boy expects to get lucky, boy unleashes ancient evil spirit, friends turn into Candarian Demons, boy fights until dawn to survive. As musical mayhem descends upon this sleepover in the woods, "camp" takes on a whole new meaning with uproarious numbers like "All the Men in my Life Keep Getting Killed by Candarian Demons," "Look Who's Evil Now" and "Do the Necronomicon."

Outer Critics Circle nomination for
Outstanding New Off-Broadway Musical

"The next Rocky Horror Show!"
- New York Times

"A ridiculous amount of fun."
- Variety

"Wickedly campy good time."
- Associated Press

Printed in the USA
CPSIA information can be obtained
at www.ICGtesting.com
LVHW010218120724
785320LV00005B/287